Jewish
COMEDY STARS

Classic to Cutting Edge

BY NORMAN H. FINKELSTEIN

KAR-BEN
PUBLISHING

For Tova and Joseph, who wonder where Saba's corny jokes come from. —N. H. F.

Kar-Ben Publishing
A division of Lerner Publishing Group, Inc.
241 First Avenue North
Minneapolis, MN 55401 U.S.A.

Website address: www.karben.com

Library of Congress Cataloging-in-Publication Data]

Finkelstein, Norman H.
    Jewish comedy stars : classic to cutting edge / by Norman H. Finkelstein.
        p.   cm.
    Includes bibliographical references and index.
    ISBN 978–0–8225–9942–5 (pbk. : alk. paper)
        1. Jews in the performing arts—United States—Biography—Juvenile literature.
    2. Jewish entertainers—United States—Biography—Juvenile literature. 3. Jewish
    comedians—United States—Biography—Juvenile literature. I. Title.
    PN1590.J48F56 2010
    792.702'80923924073—dc22   2008033478

Manufactured in the United States of America
1 – VI – 12/15/09

TABLE OF CONTENTS

INTRODUCTION

Humor has been an integral part of Jewish tradition since biblical times. When Isaac was born to aging parents—his father was more than one hundred years old and his mother in her nineties—he was named Yitzhak, the Hebrew word for "laughter." "God has brought me laughter; everyone who hears will laugh with me!" his mother, Sarah, exclaimed. Since then humor has sustained Jews by helping them cope with times of joy or adversity.

The joyous holiday of Purim celebrates the saving of the Jewish population in ancient Persia. It is observed with *shpiels*—humorous plays based on the biblical book of Esther. In eastern Europe, a tradition of humorous self-mocking folktales developed.

When Jews in large numbers began coming to the United States in the last part of the nineteenth century, they brought not only the Chelm stories with them but also a rich legacy of humor that became the foundation of American popular comedy. They also brought a rich tradition of using humorous language to express their feelings as well as self-mocking jokes to deflect the anti-Semitism they frequently experienced. The comedian Lenny Bruce once said that being Jewish is not only a religion but "a state of mind, a condition, a way of looking at the world." It is this humor, some say, that helped Jews survive years of suffering.

Why so many Jewish men and women have played important roles in the world of American comedy has been debated for years. Whether on the stage, on the radio and television, in film, or behind the scenes as writers, they have been strongly represented. Some think that humor evolved as a hereditary antidote to the centuries of hardship Jews faced around the world. They used humor to lighten their own lives.

In America, the children of Jewish immigrants, seeking ways to escape poverty, reworked their parent's Yiddish humor to fit the American experience and became America's most popular entertainers. In 1979 *Time* magazine estimated that although "Jews made up only 3 percent of the American population, fully 80 percent of professional comedians are Jewish." Today, the Jewish influence on American comedy continues. Moshe Waldoks, coauthor of *The Big Book of Jewish Humor*, observed, "There has been a certain acceptance of Jewish-style humor into American culture, akin to how black-generated jazz is now considered American."

How did this happen? Read on.

ACT I:
On Stage

At the end of the nineteenth and in the early twentieth century, more than two million Jewish immigrants arrived in the United States from eastern Europe. Their dreams of a land where the streets were paved with gold quickly evaporated into bleak reality. The Lower East Side of New York City, where large numbers of Jewish immigrants settled, was among the most densely populated places on Earth. Where could they find shelter? How could they support their families?

Unskilled and uncertain of the English language, they desperately searched for jobs to keep their families alive. Working conditions were terrible—many toiled long hours for low pay in garment industry sweatshops. There was little opportunity for fun. In a time without radio, television, and movies, an important escape from the drudgery of everyday life was the Yiddish theater.

Yiddish was the language of the street that united Jewish immigrants of all classes and backgrounds. The first generation of any immigrant group is by nature divided—one foot still in the Old Country and the other trying to gain a foothold in a strange society with unfamiliar language and customs. The Jewish newcomers were comforted by the familiarity of Yiddish culture that surrounded them. Yiddish newspapers and especially the theaters offered welcome relief. Jews from

Russia, Poland, or Lithuania could laugh together at the antics on the stage. But while they laughed, they saw their difficult lives mirrored in the comic scenes and jokes. What they saw on the stage made them realize their own shortcomings while motivating them to succeed in the New World.

In the Yiddish theaters of New York and other major U.S. cities, audiences could see translated Shakespeare plays, melodramatic love stories, and biblical tales. But the favorite of Yiddish theatergoers was the vaudeville format. Yiddish vaudeville, like American vaudeville theater, featured exaggerated mannerisms, ill-fitting clothing, and accented language. The humor revolved around comedians dressed in funny costumes and speaking with exaggerated Yiddish accents. To deflect that their accents were indeed Jewish, the vaudeville comedians began calling themselves "Dutch" acts. It seemed more polite. But the effect was the same.

Molly Picon, shown standing on a chair in the title role of *Schmendrick*, was a star of the Yiddish stage as well as a vaudeville favorite.

Vaudeville theaters could be found throughout the country—in large cities and small towns. The shows were made up of a dozen or more different acts ranging from musicians, magicians, acrobats and, of course, the ever popular comics. The weakest acts came first, and the shows built up to the most talented. Vaudevillians worked at perfecting their acts as they repeated them from city to city.

Many of the early Jewish performers were the children of eastern European, Yiddish-speaking immigrants. Anxious to make their way in the United States, these young people often had little patience for the free public school education that was offered. Their families were poor and needed the extra pennies young children could earn by selling newspapers or singing and dancing for pennies on street corners. It was a short distance from the streets to the hurly-burly of the vaudeville stage where the best of them could succeed beyond their wildest dreams. And only the best could survive the audiences who provided their own unwelcome comments, jeers, and tossed tomatoes. Eddie Cantor, later to become one of America's best-known comedians, once said that he pranced around the stage while singing and telling jokes to avoid being hit by rotten produce.

Yiddish theater in America was not a lasting phenomenon and began to disappear in the 1920s as the children of immigrants further assimilated into American culture. They threw off Yiddish culture and developed new ways of expressing themselves as Jewish entertainers in English-speaking, multicultural America. While their parents had been content to view comedy acts that depicted themselves—Yiddish-speaking newcomers trying to make sense of life in America—their American-born children, who grew up in an English-speaking environment, went beyond the experiences of their parents and transformed comedy for a larger American audience.

American vaudeville comedy had become an almost Jewish phenomenon. Comedians wearing fake beards and baggy pants regaled audiences with mispronounced Yiddish-accented English. Modern comedians telling stories and jokes in mangled English with thick Yiddish accents would seem most unseemly and perhaps anti-Semitic. But it was a different time. A typical dialogue by the vaudeville comedy team Joe Weber and Lew Fields provides an example.

In their play, *Whirl-i-Gig*, a daughter confesses her love for a naval hero to her father who responds with Yiddish inflection:

> The daughter says, "The captain is my idea of a hero."
> "A hero! Is dot a business? A tailor is a business, a shoemaker is a business, but a hero? Better you should marry a bookkeeper!"
> "A bookkeeper! I suppose you think the pen is mightier than the sword," the girl sneers.
> "You bet my life," says Papa Cohenski, "Could you sign checks with a sword?"

Weber and Fields are largely forgotten today. But the acts and lines they created at the end of the nineteenth and early twentieth century were borrowed by later comedians, including the often duplicated:

> "Who is that lady I saw you with last night?"
> "She ain't no lady. She's my wife."

Another famous Jewish comedy team was Joe Smith and Charlie Dale—known as Smith and Dale. They met as children on the Lower East Side in the 1880s when their bicycles collided. Their lines, too, have gone down into entertainment history to be reshaped and recycled by other comedians over time:

Doctor: "Did you have this pain before?"

Patient: "Yes."

Doctor: "Vell, you got it again!"

Vaudeville's popularity began declining with the advent of film and radio. At first, thcatergoers enjoyed an abbreviated live stage show along with a film. As theater owners reviewed the size of their payrolls and theatergoers began preferring movies, the live entertainment gradually disappeared. Vaudevillians had to find new outlets for their talents.

Beginning in the 1920s, many Jewish comedians found their

Short, rotund Joe Weber and tall, lean Lew Fields' mastery of fractured English and knockabout comedy made them one of early vaudeville's leading acts.

way to the Catskill Mountains of New York State. There, a growing collection of summer resorts began catering to Jewish families seeking escape from the heat and tumult of the cities. At first, they came just to live simply in boardinghouses and farmhouses and enjoy the fresh air. As time went by, the guests insisted on—and could afford—more than rocking chairs on the front lawns.

Eventually the dilapidated farmhouses were replaced by lavish hotels and resorts such as Grossinger's and Kutcher's,

In June 1955, Jerry Lewis and Wilbur the penguin performed in Brown's Hotel in Loch Sheldrake, New York, one of the major Borscht Belt institutions.

which became famous for their unending amounts of food and entertainment. Some of America's best-known singers, dancers, and comedians began their careers in what by then was known as the Borscht Belt, named after the beet soup from eastern Europe that frequently appeared on resort menus.

For many developing comedians, the Borscht Belt was a grueling training ground. Only the best survived to achieve fame. The comedians no longer relied on vaudeville costumes and Yiddish accents. The new immigrant phase of Jewish life was disappearing. Instead, the Borscht Belt developed a model for stand-up comedy that involved quick-thinking speech and one-liners. Comedians were playing to a different audience composed largely of second-generation, English-speaking American Jews.

In the beginning, the Borscht Belt acts consisted of out-of-work vaudevillians, but as the resorts grew, a new group of comedians appeared. At the heart of entertainment activity at each resort was the social director. The tummlers, as they were called, after a Yiddish word meaning "funmakers or noisemakers," had the job of making each and every resort guest happy—a nearly impossible task. At first, the tummlers organized employees and guests to put on amateur night shows. As the guests became more demanding, the tummlers added professional acts. Often, the tummlers themselves, fast on their feet and quick witted, regaled the audiences with their own patter and jokes and realized they could make a career in comedy. They understood their audiences and often made fun of them with barbed humor. "The food at the hotel is rotten—and the portions are so small," was a famous tummler line making fun of persnickety customers. Tummlers such as Joseph Levitch, Milton Berlinger, and Joseph Abramowitz crafted their humor at these resorts. They changed their names to Jerry Lewis, Milton Berle, and Joey Adams and became a few of America's favorite comedians.

Others who graduated from tummler to international star were Danny Kaye, Moss Hart, and Phil Silvers. Their name changes were important back in the 1920s and 1930s for Jews trying to get ahead in an America where anti-Semitism was still widespread. The story is told that Joey Adams once met a member of the old-line Boston Adams family who inquired if they were both related. Adams responded, "I don't know. What was your name before you changed it?"

Biographies

Morey Amsterdam

Born: December 14, 1908, Chicago, Illinois
Died: October 27, 1996, Los Angeles, California

My neighborhood is so exclusive even the police have an unlisted number.

Like other Jewish comics, Amsterdam's career began in vaudeville. His father was a concert violinist, and in 1922, young Morey went on the stage playing the cello to accompany his piano-playing brother. When Morey realized that his "off the cuff" jokes were getting more applause than his music, he turned exclusively to comedy. He was famous for the ability to quickly generate a joke on any subject at any time and became known as the Human Joke Machine.

Morey Amsterdam is best remembered for his role as Buddy Sorrell in the popular 1960s television series, *The Dick Van Dyke Show*, in which he played a comedy writer. In many ways, he was playing himself—including references to being Jewish.

Fanny Brice

Born: October 29, 1891, New York, New York
Died: May 29, 1951, Hollywood, California
Real name: Fania Borach

Your audience gives you everything you need. They tell you. There is no director who can direct like an audience.

Like many other Jewish comedians of her time, Fanny Brice left school to enter show business. After just a few years in a burlesque show, she caught the eye of legendary promoter Florenz Ziegfeld, who promptly hired her for his shows. She became a Ziegfeld Follies staple for more than twenty years. The multitalented singer and comedian became particularly associated with two hit songs. "My Man" told the story of a woman who is faithful to her husband no matter what his faults. In real life, she married three times. Her second husband, Nicky Arnstein, was a gambler who served time in jail. The other song was "Second Hand Rose," which recounted the woes of a poor girl. Fanny herself grew up in a comfortable Jewish home and had to practice Yiddish intonation to sing her first hit song written for her by Irving Berlin, "Sadie Salome, Go Home!" Singing with a Yiddish accent became her trademark. After her successful career as a comic singer on the stage, she moved her Yiddish

13

inflections to Hollywood and became the first woman to star in a sound film. In the early years of radio, Fanny re-created the character of Baby Snooks, a wisecracking toddler she originally introduced in the Follies. From its start in 1938, the *Baby Snooks* program became a weekly favorite throughout the country for over ten years. No longer relying on a Yiddish accent, Fanny played a bratty kid. She once remarked that "Snooks is just the kid I used to be. . . . With all her deviltry, she is still a good kid, never vicious or mean." Her life was immortalized in the film, *Funny Girl*, with Barbra Streisand playing the role of Fanny.

George Jessel

Born: April 3, 1898, New York, New York
Died: May 23, 1981, Los Angeles, California

The human brain starts working the moment you are born and never stops until you stand up to speak in public.

George Jessel was known as the Toastmaster General of the United States, an unofficial title given to him by President Franklin Delano Roosevelt in recognition of the hundreds of speeches given by Jessel in support of social and political causes. His reputation for public speaking led to his becoming a popular deliverer of eulogies at the funerals of well-know entertainers.

As a child, he sang on street corners to earn money for his family after his father died. His big break into show business occurred in 1910 when he joined Gus Edwards's traveling vaudeville act, which featured other talented boys and girls. Later, he created a comedy monologue called "Hello, Mama," which became popular with theatergoers for decades. Using a prop telephone, he pretended to talk to his mother about a variety of topics that featured Jewish humor. He starred in Broadway shows, including *The Jazz Singer*, his most popular role. Yet, when the play was turned into the first talking motion picture, Al Jolson got to play the role that Jessel originated since the studio refused to meet his salary demands. Jessel was a film producer and the star of his own radio and television show in the early 1950s.

Molly Picon

Born: June 1, 1898, New York, New York
Died: April 6, 1992, Lancaster, Pennsylvania
Real name: Margaret Pyekoon

All I hope is that I've gladdened your hearts too, and brightened your lives as you have mine.

Although short of stature, Molly Picon was a giant on the stage in the Yiddish theater, in film, and on Broadway. Born on the Lower East Side of New York, she first appeared onstage when she was five years old. She grew up in Philadelphia where, as a teenager, she dropped out of high school to perform in Yiddish vaudeville. In 1919, as part of a troupe playing in Boston, she fell in love with Jacob Kalich, the manager of the Boston Grand Opera House. Kalich became Molly's husband as well as her professional partner. Together, they created memorable comedic and musical Yiddish plays, which became the favorite of Jewish theatergoers throughout the United States. They traveled to Europe, where Molly not only learned from other Yiddish-speaking performers but also became a star whose fame spread back to the United States. Molly was particularly beloved for her lively and funny characterizations of young women disguised as boys. Her sense of humor was revealed in popular plays including *Yankele* and *Mamele* in the 1920s. In a *New York Times* review of *Here Runs the Bride*, William Schack wrote that Molly is "among the comparatively few musical-comedy players whose artistry transcends their immediate personalities. She can take off male and female, young and old, the rowdy and the refined."

By the 1930s, she starred in comic Yiddish films that were produced in Europe, including the classic *Yiddle Mitn Fiddle*. Those films actually provide us with glimpses into *shtetl* life in Europe that was destroyed during the Holocaust. Her talents took her beyond the limited world of Yiddish onto the American stage and in films. In 1963 she starred in *Milk and Honey*, a Broadway musical about Israel. Her memorable film roles include *Come Blow Your Horn*, for which she received an Oscar nomination, and *Fiddler on the Roof*. She also appeared on a number of television shows. As the world of Yiddish theater disappeared, Molly continued to travel around the country into her eighties, entertaining Jewish and non-Jewish audiences.

Smith and Dale

Joe Smith

Born: February 16, 1884, New York, New York
Died: February 22, 1981, New York, New York
Real name: Joseph Sultzer

Charlie Dale

Born: September 6, 1885, New York, New York
Died: November 16, 1971, New York, New York
Real name: Charles Marks

Joe Smith *(left)* and Charlie Dale *(right)*

Like other Jewish comedians of their time, Smith and Dale grew up in the Yiddish-speaking world of the Lower East Side. They developed a comedy act when they were teenagers, and, by the early 1900s, became well known on the vaudeville stage with their comedy sketches performed with Yiddish accents. They also appeared together in a number of short comedy films and made appearances on early television variety shows. In the 1920s, their sketch, *Doctor Kronkheit and His Only Living Patient* became a staple vaudeville act, and many of the dialogues are still used by comedians today.

"Doctor, it hurts when I do this."
"Don't do that."

Weber and Fields

Joseph Weber

Born: August 11, 1867, New York, New York
Died: May 10, 1942, Los Angeles, California

Lew Fields

Born: January 1, 1867, New York, New York
Died: July 20, 1941, Los Angeles, California
Real name: Lewis Schanfield

Weber and Fields met as students in elementary school. They didn't last long there and were expelled when they were eleven years old. Both came from very poor families and set out on a show business career together. They developed a "Dutch" act, speaking Yiddish-accented English and dressing in oversized clothes. Their act was action packed. They chased each other around the stage, slapping each other while keeping up a fast-paced patter of jokes and one-liners.

Lew Fields (*left*) and Joseph Weber (*right*)

Their entrance theme song was appropriately named, "Here We Are, a Jolly Pair." As their act became noticed, they received bookings across the country and improved on their act as they traveled. Their comic parodies of well-known stage plays were particularly popular and attracted attention from theater critics and audiences alike.

A man goes to a psychiatrist. The doctor says, "You're crazy." The man says, "I want a second opinion." "OK, you're ugly too!"

Henny Youngman

Born: March 16, 1906, Liverpool, England
Died: February 24, 1998, New York, New York

Unlike other comedians, Youngman did not believe in long, drawn-out stories or skits in his act. Rather, he focused strictly on quick punch lines and insults delivered in rapid-fire sequence. Thus he earned the title King of the One-Liners, bestowed on him early in his career by news columnist Walter Winchell.

Youngman grew up in Brooklyn, New York. He took violin lessons and his parents envisioned a career for him as a classical violinist. Their wishes never materialized although he nearly always appeared on stage holding his violin. He didn't like school and spent more time at local theaters than in classrooms. He worked as a printer and later at a S. S. Kresge five-and-ten-cent store where he met his wife, Sadie. He began his show business career leading a small band called the Swanee Syncopators but soon discovered he could attract more attention as a stand-up comic. He took his act to nightclubs, private parties, and radio and television programs throughout his long career. Like other Jewish comedians, he worked at resorts in the Catskills. There he began perfecting his one-liners by insulting customers. "Someday you'll go far, and I hope you stay there." His big break occurred in 1937 when he first performed on Kate Smith's popular radio show. For the next two years, he was a regular on the program and his popularity grew. Using his violin as a prop, he amazed audiences with his rapid-fire delivery of one-liners, insults and gags. He was a hard worker who never turned down a job, no matter how big or small whether it was before an audience of thousands at a prestigious Las Vegas hotel or a Bar Mitzvah celebration with 150 guests. Youngman appeared in several movies and wrote a number of books including his 1973 autobiography, *Take My Wife, Please!* Sadie, his wife of nearly sixty years, was good natured about being the butt of many insults. ("I miss my wife's cooking—as often as I can." "My wife will buy anything marked down. She brought home two dresses and an escalator." "I take my wife everywhere, but she always finds her way home.") Even as he grew older, he never missed an opportunity to stand before a crowd. "If I can still make someone laugh, then I must be alive."

Toward the end of his career, Henny occasionally appeared as a guest on television talk and variety shows. One of the classic one-liners in American comedy remains his insulting quip, "Take my wife—please!"

ACT II:
On Air

Vaudeville began dying in the 1920s. Initially it was due to the fast-developing film industry and then, by the end of the decade, the poverty of the Great Depression (1929–1942). In an attempt to save vaudeville, live entertainment and movies began sharing the same bill. But gradually, films outlived the last of the vaudeville acts. Vaudeville houses around the country closed or were transformed into movie theaters.

The most successful vaudeville entertainers moved first to radio in the 1930s and 1940s and then to television in the 1950s. By 1930 the number of American families owning radios had grown to well over thirteen million. David Sarnoff, chairman of the board of RCA and instrumental in NBC color broadcasts, stated that radio was "creating a new common fund of experience and information that was democratic in its touch-of-the-dial accessibility."

When the United States was in the grip of the Great Depression, something was needed to lift the spirits of the American people. Americans needed to laugh. Radio listenership had dropped dramatically as people tired of the old music programming of the late 1920s. The networks looked for something new to bring back listeners. Vaudeville comics found themselves in great demand for radio. Soon well-known stage comedians including Eddie Cantor, Jack Benny, and George Burns became instant hits on radio.

The radio was the family's entertainment center until it was replaced by television in the 1950s.

One of the most popular carryovers of Dutch acts to radio was Jack Pearl in his role as Baron Munchausen. As the baron told tall tales, his partner Charlie would deflate them. The baron then responded in a thick Yiddish accent with, "Vas you dere, Sharlie?" and the audience would roar with delight. Soon many Americans were using the expression. These acts largely disappeared when the Nazis came to power in Germany in the 1930s. Yiddish-accented Jews making fun of themselves was no longer appropriate.

Radio captured the hearts of Americans. In an era of national crazes from flagpole sitting to marathon dancing, radio served as the instant dispenser of the latest fads. The family radio was more than a piece of furniture. It was a magical link to an enchanted world of free entertainment. It provided shared experiences to everyone, rich and poor, city dweller and farmer, black and white, educated and illiterate. Radio made its performers into national heroes. By the end of World War II (1939–1945), more American homes had radios than bathtubs.

Because of their widespread traveling, successful vaudeville comics had developed styles of humor that played well in all parts of the country. They were experienced men and women who had learned their craft under the most trying conditions. Simply to have survived the demanding audiences was a sign of competence and accomplishment. They loved their lives as comics, and it showed when they performed.

Comedians tried to create new presentations for their audiences, but the best comics kept their gags and stories simple. They knew from experience that nothing turned an audience off more quickly than a complicated story or an insincere delivery. Once on the radio, they learned to present their material without relying on the sight gags that had sustained them on the stage. This meant no more funny costumes, suggestive winks, grimaces, or hand motions that had made theater audiences laugh.

But old habits die hard. One well-known comedian, Ed Wynn, insisted on doing his radio show wearing the same makeup and costumes he used in vaudeville. He performed his radio show in front of a live audience because he depended on the reactions of people in the studio to make his gags come alive. In a review of Wynn's first radio broadcast in 1932, one listener underestimated the comedian's need to perform in front of an audience: "This ever funny clown, of course, does not come into the category of those who have to be seen in order to be fully appreciated." Little did that listener know about what was actually taking place in the studio! When television overtook radio, Ed Wynn's outlandish outfits could be viewed in homes all across the country.

In a direct carryover from vaudeville, radio comedians relied on a second person on their programs to act as the straight man, or stooge, for jokes, gags, and scenes. The stooge generally took one of three characterizations. First were the wives, often the comedians' real spouses. The most famous husband-and-wife teams were George Burns and Gracie Allen and Jack Benny and Mary Livingston. A second category consisted of foreign-accented stooges like Bert Gordon's Mad Russian on *The Eddie Cantor Show* and Artie Auerbach's Mr. Kitzel on *The Jack Benny Program.* Both used Yiddish inflections and accents. Finally, there were the program announcers, many of whom were associated with particular comedians and programs for years. Jack Benny's longtime announcer was Don Wilson. For Ed Wynn, that announcer was Graham McNamee with whom he traded lively barbs.

Ed Wynn *(right)* **exchanges one-liners with straight man Graham McNamee on the popular radio show,** *The Fire Chief,* **1936.**

These early pioneers invented their on-air styles as they went along. The medium was so new, there were no established rules. Jack Benny, for example, realized that while other comedians were running out of their old vaudeville jokes, he introduced skits based on popular books and movies and on his own fictional life outside the broadcast. "Our sketches were the first real satires in radio," he later recounted. Benny was also the first radio comedian to use other cast members to highlight his fictional characteristics of stinginess and vanity, traits that made him the butt of many jokes.

While the audience and his cast easily recognized his faults, Benny's radio personality never admitted to any. His eyes were perfect baby blue, his age an eternal thirty-nine, and his violin playing of concert-hall excellence. In real life, he was an accomplished violinist, but one of the ongoing gags dealt with his terrible violin skills. Poor Professor LeBlanc, his violin teacher (played by Mel Blanc, the voice of Bugs Bunny), would accompany Benny's scale exercises with rhyming insults, which his student never seemed to hear: "Make the notes a little thinner./ I don't want to lose my dinner."

A number of the popular Jewish radio comedians were graduates of vaudeville or the Borscht Belt. They had learned their craft the hard way, in front of very opinionated and critical audiences. As they made the shift from vaudeville and the Borscht Belt, their humor became less focused on Jewish themes, but the skills and strategies learned onstage remained.

The popularity of the Catskill resorts peaked in the 1950s when Jewish vacationers began heading to other destinations, especially Florida. The comedians, however, thrived on radio and later, on television. Jewish comedians, who had mainly appeared before Jewish audiences, were faced with a dilemma. To succeed on radio and television they needed to appeal to a broad audience scattered around the entire country. The challenge was to remake their jokes and acts in ways that did not reduce the intensity of their performances. But it is always difficult to completely erase your past. Jack Benny's programs, while seemingly without direct Jewish content, introduced Yiddish-accented Mr. Kitzel and periodic ad-libs gave a nod to his Jewish heritage. Once, when someone mentioned the real name of a well-known movie star on the air, Benny quickly ad-libbed, "My name was Benjamin Kubelsky!" The audience roared with laughter not realizing that Benny was telling the truth.

The shift of home entertainment from radio to television was not as difficult as one would have expected. Experimenters had been working for years on ways to broadcast pictures and sound. David Sarnoff, the founder of NBC, was himself a Jewish immigrant from Russia. At the 1939 World's Fair in New York, Sarnoff revealed the first large-scale public demonstration of a new medium—television. But it took television until after World War II to take hold. Just as early radio personalities drew from their vaudeville roots, the early television stars came from radio. Milton Berle's popular *Texaco Star Theater* led to the sale of millions of new television sets as neighbor began telling neighbor about the wildly comical show. His popularity was so great, he was given the title Mr. Television.

The 1950s brought an increase in the number and type of comedy shows. The variety shows evolved from the Borscht Belt one-liners and slapstick of Milton Berle to more sophisticated written skits. Sid Caesar's *Your Show of Shows* (1950–1954) featured funny sketches that often involved the use of Yiddish expressions. Although most viewers chuckled at the strange words, they hadn't the slightest idea of their meanings. Jewish viewers, however, felt an immediate connection to the "inside jokes," and it made them proud. Even as Yiddish was dying out as a spoken language among Jews, Yiddish expressions and words like *schlep* and *oy* became popular among non-Jews as a

The majority of successful Jewish radio comics were able to make the transition to television during the 1950s.

result of Jewish television comics. Sid Caesar surrounded himself with some of the best-known names in entertainment—singers, dancers, and actors. But it was his own appearance in funny skits that made the show popular with viewers. They enjoyed his flexible facial contortions and double-talking wisecracks.

In 1993 Neil Simon, who became one of America's most honored playwrights, wrote a Broadway play, *Laughter on the 23rd Floor.* It was based on his experiences working with other talented writers, among them Woody Allen and Mel Brooks, week after week to create Sid Caesar's program. When the writers, nearly all of them Jewish, reached an impasse with a show deadline looming—the programs were all aired live—the lead writer, Mel Tolkin, would shout, "Gentlemen, we've got to get something done! Jews all over America will be watching Saturday night!"

Two groups of over-the-top comedians made their mark in

popular films. The Marx Brothers and the Three Stooges were not graduates of the Borscht Belt. Instead, their fame grew in Hollywood after learning their skills on the vaudeville stage.

In the 1940s, at the end of World War II, a Jewish gangster, Benjamin "Bugsy" Siegel laid the groundwork that transformed Las Vegas, a dusty desert town in Nevada, into a gambling and entertainment center. Only the best-known singers and comedians were hired to lure customers to the glamorous casino hotels. Joey Bishop, Rodney Dangerfield, Jackie Mason, and Don Rickles became Las Vegas nightclub favorites with their confrontational and sometimes insulting brands of humor.

Perhaps the biggest boost to comedy in general and Jewish comedians in particular began in the 1970s with the beginning of television's *Saturday Night Live*. Many of the writers and stars were Jewish, and they were proud to present sketches and characters with obvious Jewish connections and themes. Gilda Radner's imitation of an out-of-control Jewish woman shopper created furor from Jewish groups, but it was all in good fun and appreciated by viewers.

At a time when Jewish children felt like outsiders during the Christmas season, comedian Jon Lovitz created the character of Hanukkah Harry on *Saturday Night Live* as a Santa Claus replacement. Most popular of all were the changing versions of Adam Sandler's "Hanukkah Song" and the release of *Eight Crazy Nights*, an animated film based on the song. Hanukkah music has never been the same.

The journey of Jewish American comedy has come a long way since its start in Yiddish theater over a century ago. As it changed to fit new times and new technologies, "many Americans had, across the decades, been absorbing a Jewish sensibility as they laughed at Jewish comedians." These Jewish comedians created the models for modern television sitcoms, humorous films, and comedy clubs.

Biographies

Woody Allen

Born: December 1, 1935, New York, New York
Real name: Allen Stewart Konigsberg

It's not that I'm afraid to die; I just don't want to be there when it happens.

Woody Allen is best known for directing films and his acting portrayals of nervous, paranoid characters. He grew up in Brooklyn, New York, and like other Jewish comedians of his time, he was happier on the streets with friends than in the classroom. An avid reader of comic books and listener to popular radio programs, he developed a quirky sense of humor that led to a career as a writer of jokes and one-liners. His talent was honed when he worked as one of the staff writers for Sid Caesar's *Your Show of Shows*. That early television show featured other writers such as

Mel Brooks and Carl Reiner, who went on to comedy careers of their own. While working as a comedian in nightclubs, Allen developed an image that became his "calling card"—a nerdy, insecure paranoid. Along the way, he also became a noted jazz musician. His greatest professional accomplishments were in film. He directed and starred in a large number of popular films, each playing to his own unique talents and personality. His best-known films include *Annie Hall* (1977), *Zelig* (1983), *Broadway Danny Rose* (1984), *Radio Days* (1987), *Bullets Over Broadway* (1994), and *Vicky Christina Barcelona* (2008).

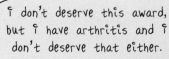

i don't deserve this award, but i have arthritis and i don't deserve that either.

Jack Benny

Born: February 14, 1894, Waukegan, Illinois,
Died: December 26, 1974, Beverly Hills, California
Real name: Benjamin Kubelsky

Jack Benny did not enter show business as a comedian. In fact, he did not enter it as Jack Benny. He was the son of immigrant Jewish parents from Lithuania. Unlike many other Jewish comedians of his era who were raised in large-city ghetto slums such as New York's Lower East Side, Benny grew up in Waukegan, Illinois, where his father operated a men's clothing store. His parents wanted him to become a professional violinist and paid for him to take lessons from a classical music teacher in Chicago, but the young man had other ideas. A poor student, he was expelled from high school in the ninth grade. At the age of seventeen, he took his violin talents into a local theater where he played in the pit orchestra for three years. When the theater closed in 1912, he went on the vaudeville circuit. To the delight of audiences, he began inserting humor into his act, and before long, the violin became a stage prop. Benny said: "The audience laughed. The sound intoxicated me. That laughter ended my days as a musician." Changing his name after leaving the U.S. Navy after World War I (1914–1918), he moved with ease to the top of the vaudeville world. In 1924 he starred at the Palace Theater in New York and two years later appeared in a Broadway play, *Great Temptations*. In 1927 he married Sadie Marks, who he first met when her cousins, the Marx Brothers, invited him to a family Passover seder while they were touring together in Vancouver, Canada. His radio career began in 1932, and *The Jack Benny Program* eventually became the most popular show in the United States. At a time when other radio comedians were running out of their old vaudeville jokes, Benny discovered a nearly inexhaustible source of material by introducing skits based on his own fictional life outside of the broadcast. He surrounded himself with a cast that remained his "gang" for decades moving easily from radio to television. His wife played the role of Benny's girlfriend, Mary Livingston. On the air, he assumed the character of a vain, stingy, and conceited person who was the constant target of his cast members. His programs were tightly scripted by talented writers, and Benny became known for his keen ability to use timing and key catchphrases to paint images in the listeners' minds. His use of "Well!" in response to unflattering comments became one of his most popular phrases. Another was, "I'm thinking it over!" which first appeared in a sketch called, "Your Money or Your Life." The writers were stumped: They could not think of a way for Benny to respond to a robber. One writer began nagging a second, who just sat quietly without responding. After a while, somewhat annoyed, the silent writer yelled, "Stop nagging. I'm thinking it over!" When Benny read the line on the air after a suspenseful pause, the radio skit became part of broadcasting history. The radio show was on the air until 1955. He entered television in 1950, modeling his show on the successful radio series.

Milton Berle

Born: July 12, 1908, New York, New York
Died: March 27, 2002, Los Angeles, California
Real name: Milton Berlinger

Under the influence of his mother, Milton Berle, then Berlinger, became a child actor in silent films at the age of five. He changed his name when he was sixteen years old. His first stage appearance was in the 1920 production of the Broadway hit play, *The Florodora Girl*, which shaped his reputation as an up-and-coming comedian. He went on to star in the Ziegfeld Follies and on the vaudeville stage. While admired by other comedians, he was often accused of "borrowing" jokes from them. He once joked, "I listened to Jack Benny on the radio last night. He was so funny I dropped my pad and pencil." By the end of his life, it was said that his joke file was the largest ever known, possibly more than nine hundred thousand. He hosted a number of radio shows in the 1930s and 1940s and was a frequent guest on other programs. His last radio series quickly evolved into his Tuesday night television blockbuster.

There aren't many people who become known by a type of broadcast medium. Milton Berle has gone down in history as Mr. Television. All but forgotten by new generations, Berle is credited with single-handedly making the fledgling television industry an early success. Television was a new phenomenon in 1948 when NBC brought Milton Berle to the small black-and-white screen. His *Texaco Star Theater* was a radio success, and the move of his program to television allowed the former vaudeville comic to bring some of his outrageous visual acting to life. His jokes were corny, and the costumes he wore on the air varied from caveman to clown. "Good evening, Ladies and Germs," he would say, and the audience would roar with laughter. His program was such an instant hit that television sales skyrocketed. Around the country, things seemed to come to a standstill on Tuesday evenings at eight when, it was estimated, four out every five American televisions were tuned to the *Texaco Star Theater*. Restaurants and theaters complained about business slowdowns. Families without televisions joined friends who owned sets to watch and laugh. Berle earned another nickname when he told watching children at the end of one 1949 show, "Listen to your Uncle Miltie and go to bed." Uncle Miltie became Americans' favorite uncle to viewers of all ages.

As television comedy grew more sophisticated, his popularity sagged, and his program was canceled. From that point in the late 1950s, his television appearances were limited to guest spots on other programs. But that was not the end of his career. He appeared in nightclubs and starred in a number of popular films including *It's a Mad, Mad, Mad, Mad World* (1963) and Woody Allen's *Broadway Danny Rose* in which he played himself.

Joey Bishop

Son of a gun!

Born: February 3, 1918, New York, New York
Died: October 17, 2007, Newport Beach, California
Real name: Joseph Abraham Gottlieb

Joey Bishop was the last surviving member of the Rat Pack, the close-knit group of entertainers surrounding legendary singer Frank Sinatra. They performed together in Las Vegas nightclubs, on television shows, and in films such as *Ocean's Eleven* and *Sergeants 3*. The group included Dean Martin and Sammy Davis Jr. Growing up in Philadelphia, Joey entertained his friends with imitations of famous actors. He dropped out of high school at the age of sixteen. Then he changed his name and went on the road with two friends performing a comedy act. He served in the U.S. Army during World War II and upon his discharge developed a comedy act of his own, which eventually took him into early television. He appeared in his own shows and was a frequent guest on other programs. He entertained with the Rat Pack and was easily recognizable since he was the least showy of the group and became famous for keeping a straight face during the antics of the others.

Mel Brooks

Born: June 28, 1926, Brooklyn, New York
Real name: Melvin Kaminsky

As a short and nonathletic child, Mel Brooks learned to deflect bullying with humor. Like others, his rise to fame began in the Catskill Mountains, where as a teenager he washed dishes and observed the comedians who worked there. He began to develop his own comedy act, but his fledgling career was delayed by World War II. After serving in Europe, he returned to the Catskills, elevated to the position of social director. At one of the hotels, he befriended another comedian, Sid Caesar, and when Caesar entered television in the early 1950s, Brooks became one of the highly talented writers who wrote *Your Show of Shows*. His sense of humor was often misunderstood. He was never shy about being outrageous. One of his first successes was a record album he recorded with fellow Jewish comedian Carl Reiner, *The 2000 Year Old Man* (1960), in which he parodied historical events through the funny ad-libbed observations of a man who was an improbable eyewitness to the world's great events. The old gentleman used a Yiddish-inflected accent to complain that over the years he had more than forty-two thousand children "and not one comes to visit me." Using a similar theme, he wrote, produced, and acted in another historical spoof, *History of the World: Part 1*. Two of his greatest film successes, *Young Frankenstein* (1974) and *The Producers* (1968) became equally popular Broadway hits with the addition of music composed by Brooks himself. His comic genius sometimes offended people because of its insensitivity. "Springtime for Hitler" was the only song in the film version of *The Producers*, to which Brooks added other colorful songs to create the musical stage play. Brooks has the distinction of being one of the few to receive awards in multiple categories,

Humor is just another defense against the universe.

having won Oscar, Grammy, and Tony awards for his works. The Broadway play *The Producers* (2001) holds the distinction of claiming the most Tonys ever awarded—twelve.

George Burns

Born: January 20, 1896, New York, New York
Died: March 9, 1996, Beverly Hills, California
Real name: Nathan Birnbaum

Nathan Birnbaum grew up in poverty. With the death of his father in 1903, he went to work in a candy store at the age of seven. There, he met other young boys his age and to while away the time, they began singing songs in harmony. They eventually realized they could make more money singing on street corners for pennies than they could working in the store. The Peewee Quartet launched young "Nattie" in show business. Never a good student, he left school in the fourth grade to seek a life in show business and changed his name to George Burns. He tried a number of different acts, from roller skating to dancing, but real success eluded him until 1923 when he met and eventually married Gracie Allen. They teamed up and developed an act in which Gracie asked questions and George provided comical answers. When George realized that his wife was actually funnier, they reversed roles, and George Burns became the most famous straight man in radio. Gracie, characterized as a pleasant but dim-witted wife, made the most illogical events seem completely understandable. They were a vaudeville hit and ultimately played the Palace Theater in New York. They married in 1926. They made several movies together, but their real success was first on radio and then on television. Their programs went through different stages until they hit the right formula in the 1940s with *The George Burns and Gracie Allen Show*. Like Jack Benny in his own program, they portrayed a fictional form of their own lives as entertainers. When the show moved to television in 1950, it evolved into a situation comedy with George often going out of character to speak directly to the audience about what was happening in the program. After Gracie's death in 1964, George tried out other program ideas, but none was as successful as the original. He then began a new aspect of his life by starring in a number of successful films including *The*

Sunshine Boys (1975), for which he, at the age of eighty, received an Academy Award for Best Supporting Actor and a series of *Oh, God!* films. His age became a running gag until his death at the age of one hundred. He often quipped, "At my age, I don't buy green bananas."

Sid Caesar

Born: September 8, 1922, Yonkers, New York

Sid Caesar was another versatile entertainer who got his start in the Borscht Belt. He worked in a number of the Catskill Mountain resorts as a musician and comedian. While serving in the U.S. Coast Guard during World War II, he helped create camp shows at the base in which he also performed. His ease onstage and keen ability to ad-lib jokes and stories made him very popular. After the war, Sid first tried working in Hollywood but quickly found his way back to New York where he appeared in a

The guy who invented the first wheel was an idiot. The guy who invented the other three—HE was a genius.

Broadway musical and began what was to become a television career. Sid Caesar is best remembered for *Your Show of Shows*, which debuted in 1950. A Saturday night variety program hosted by Caesar, it was incredibly popular with viewers of all ages. Although it was only on the air for four years, the program had an important impact on television comedy. It aired live for ninety minutes a week, putting tremendous pressure on the cast to get everything right the first—and only—time. Needless to say, Caesar had to rely on instantaneous ad-libs to cover up anything that went wrong. Working with his talented writers and a superb cast of character actors, including Imogene Coca, Caesar's sketches relied heavily on facial expressions, exaggerated foreign accents, and improbable situations. The sketches set a standard for sophisticated satire that set them apart from other comedy shows of the time. In one skit, Caesar is dressed in what appears to be a European army officer's bemedaled uniform. As an "assistant" helps arrange the appearance of the uniform and its medals, the officer bellows a series of orders using Yiddish (or German) words—*geschmutzik* (dirty) eyeglasses, or *shpritzen* (spraying) perfume. The final scene, which evoked much audience laughter, reveals that the officer is actually a uniformed New York City apartment building doorman who hails a cab for a tenant.

Your Show of Shows was followed by *Caesar's Hour*. It focused on satirical skits poking fun at popular movies and television shows while providing Caesar countless opportunities to ad-lib. His skit, "The Professor," in which he portrayed a less-than-knowledgeable expert, provided Mel Brooks with the idea for *The 2,000 Year Old Man*. Caesar remained on television and branched out into film by the 1960s. He starred, with other leading comedians of the time, in the hit film comedy *It's a Mad, Mad, Mad, Mad World* and played irreverent Coach Calhoun in the musical film *Grease* (1979).

Eddie Cantor

Born: January 31, 1892, New York, New York
Died: October 10, 1964, Hollywood, California
Real name: Israel Iskowitz

Many of the most successful Jewish comedians in the early twentieth century grew up in poverty, the children of Yiddish-speaking immigrants to the United States. Often, it was pure chance that led them to their careers, while some of their friends headed for lives of crime. Eddie

> He hasn't an enemy in the world—but all his friends hate him.

Cantor came very close to becoming a juvenile delinquent, but a summer camp experience turned his life toward the stage. Eddie was raised by his Yiddish-speaking grandmother, unfamiliar with American ways, who quickly lost control of her streetwise, cocky grandson. He received his real education on the streets where he grew up singing and dancing for coins on street corners. After leaving school, he changed his name to Eddie Cantor and found a job as a singing waiter in a saloon. From there, he joined Gus Edwards's Kid Kabaret, a theater company of talented boys and girls. Cantor went on to perform in vaudeville where he developed a unique style. It included prancing around the stage at a fast pace, clapping his hands, and goggling his eyes, all the while singing and joking to the delight of the audience. He claimed later that he adopted that constantly moving style to avoid the fruits and vegetables often thrown at entertainers by less-than-satisfied ticket holders. He frequently appeared onstage to sing and dance in black face and used a Yiddish accent in telling jokes. He was discovered by showman Florenz Ziegfeld, who hired him to appear in his Follies shows on Broadway. Cantor quickly became a favorite of audiences. He went on to star in popular films in the late 1920s and 1930s including *Kid from Spain* (1932) and *Kid Millions* (1934). In 1942 he starred in a film called *Banjo Eyes*, titled for his trademarked popping eyes. His radio career began in 1931. With the arrival of television, he moved effortlessly into that medium. Cantor was known for his philanthropy, particularly his work on behalf of the March of Dimes, which he helped found to eradicate polio. His support for Israel earned him that nation's special Medal of Valor. He married his childhood sweetheart, Ida. Together they had five daughters, who were often mentioned on his broadcasts.

Rodney Dangerfield

Born: November 22, 1921, Babylon, New York
Died: October 5, 2004, Los Angeles, California
Real name: Jacob Cohen

"I don't get no respect." With that one little sentence, Rodney Dangerfield went down into comedy history. His father, who used the stage name of Phil Roy, was a vaude-villian who left the family when Rodney was a small child. Poor and taunted by anti-Semitism at school, Rodney responded by writing jokes. As he grew older, he began performing at theater amateur nights under the name of Jack Roy. Like other comedi-ans, he worked in the Borscht Belt. His entry into the real world of entertainment occurred years later when, under the name he would soon make famous, Rodney Dangerfield, he appeared in comedy

My wife and i were happy for twenty years. Then we met.

clubs and began attracting attention. What followed were guest spots on television shows where his adopted personality as a man who got no respect got laughs. He opened his own comedy club, Dangerfield's, in New York, which became a jumping-off spot for soon-to-be popular comics. He appeared in several films including *Caddyshack* (1980) and *Back to School* (1986). His recording of *No Respect* won a Grammy Award in 1981.

I wasn't born a fool. It took work to get this way.

Danny Kaye

Born: January 18, 1913, Brooklyn, New York
Died: March 3, 1987, Los Angeles, California
Real name: David Daniel Kaminsky

David Daniel Kaminsky never graduated from high school. As a teenager, he worked as a soda jerk in local drugstores. Friends who had seen him sing and dance on street corners told him that he belonged in show business. He earned his comedy education at Borscht Belt resorts in the Catskills in the 1930s. He had a knack for languages and a reputation as a fast talker. Combining both skills became a trademark for him as he regaled audiences onstage and on film with songs such as "Tchaikovsky," in which he rapidly fired off the hard-to-pronounce names of Russian composers. His professional career began in low-budget short films, which led to his first Broadway appearance in a play. Then it was off to Hollywood and starring roles in a number of successful comedies, including *The Inspector General* (1949), *The Court Jester* (1956), and *The Five Pennies* (1959). Many of the tongue-twisting songs that became associated with him were written by his wife, Sylvia Fine.

Kaye had a short-lived radio career. It seemed that his famed facial contortions so popular in films could not be seen by the radio audience. His television career was more successful. *The Danny Kaye Show* aired from 1963 to 1967, after which he frequently appeared as a guest on other programs. He had a rich life beyond the entertainment field. He was the owner of the Seattle Mariners baseball team and was an original sponsor of UNICEF and traveled around the world to educate Americans about the lives of hungry and uneducated children.

Jerry Lewis

Born: March 16, 1926, Newark, New Jersey
Real name: Joseph Levitch

For many people, Jerry Lewis symbolizes the annual Labor Day fund-raising telethon for the Muscular Dystrophy Association. His philanthropy has raised millions of dollars to find a cure for that disease. For others, it is the image of a zany, off-the-wall comic that identifies Lewis. He was born to show business parents. Even as a child, he was part of the Borscht Belt scene. His parents entertained at the summer resorts, and he got his start working there as well, inserting his own brand of humor as he waited on tables. "I never got a formal education," he once told an interviewer, "So my intellect is my common sense. I don't have anything else going for me. And my common sense opens the door to instinct." His early show business acts displayed something less than common sense. He mimicked audience members, threw dishes, and otherwise acted as if he were an out-of-control child. Audiences at first didn't know what to make of Lewis's brand of comedy. Only when he teamed up with another entertainer, Dean Martin, in 1946, did his comedy begin to attract attention. Martin

and Lewis became popular radio and television stars, but personal differences led to a breakup of their team in 1956. Lewis then went on to a successful career in film. While professional critics held negative views, theatergoers loved the films. Among the most successful, which he also directed, were *The Errand Boy* (1962) and *The Nutty Professor* (1963). His films became particularly loved in France, and in 2006, he was awarded the French Legion of Honor. In later years, even as his health declined, Lewis still found the time and stamina to raise funds for his beloved Muscular Dystrophy Association, including appearances in the yearly telethons.

The Marx Brothers

Leonard "Chico" Marx

Born: March 22, 1887, New York, New York
Died: October 11, 1961, Hollywood, California

Arthur "Harpo" Marx

Born: November 23, 1888, New York, New York
Died: September 28, 1964, Hollywood, California

Julius "Groucho" Marx

Born: October 2, 1890, New York, New York
Died: August 19, 1977, Los Angeles, California

Milton "Gummo" Marx

Born: October 23, 1897, New York, New York
Died: April 21, 1977, Palm Springs, California

Herbert "Zeppo" Marx

Born: February 25, 1901, New York, New York
Died: November 30, 1979, Palm Springs, California

It all began with their mother, Minnie, whose brother, Al Shean, was a well-known vaudeville star. With five sons to raise, she decided that show business was the key to success for her family. During the first two decades of the twentieth century, the Marx Brothers, accompanied by their ever-present mother, performed in musical and comedy acts on vaudeville circuits around the country. It was in small theaters in even smaller towns that they began perfecting their zany acts. The four older brothers received their nicknames from another vaudeville actor during a poker game in 1915. "Groucho was glum, Harpo played the harp, Chico liked chicken, Gummo wore rubbers.

From top to bottom: **Groucho, Zeppo, Harpo, Chico, and Gummo Marx**

Zeppo's nickname, selected by Groucho, means nothing." By the 1920s, Groucho became the group's wisecracking leader with Chico speaking in a fake Italian accent while silent Harpo communicated by honking a horn. Gummo left the act first to pursue other interests, while Zeppo made only occasional appearances with the other three brothers. Groucho, Harpo, and Chico created their own niche in the history of comedy. Their films, filled with fast-talking wise-cracks, double meanings, and frenzied action, were not as popular with audiences at first as they would later become. Their Broadway play *Cocoanuts* (1925) was turned into a film in 1929 and was the model for the films that fol-lowed. Although all the films were scripted, Groucho pretty much ad-libbed his way through them with hilarious puns and one-liners. Some of their best-known films are *Horse Feathers* (1932), *Duck Soup* (1933), and *A Night at the Opera* (1935). The brothers eventually went on separate paths with Groucho becoming the most successful. His unique mustache, raised eyebrows, and ever-present cigar were his visual trademarks. His classic one-liners became famous. "I don't want to belong to any club that will accept me as a member." "Last night I shot an elephant in my pajamas and how he got in my pajamas I'll never know." "I never forget a face, but in your case I'll be glad to make an excep-tion." He began appearing on radio, first as a guest on the shows of others and later on his own programs. His quiz show, *You Bet Your Life*, became an instant radio and later television hit from 1947 until 1961. Unlike today's game shows, the focus was not on guests winning things but on Groucho himself who ad-libbed his way to laughs, usu-ally at the expense of contestants. When one woman gave her age as "approaching forty," Groucho responded, "From which direction?"

Jackie Mason

Born: June 9, 1934, Sheboygan, Wisconsin
Real name: Yacov Moshe Maza

i have enough money to last me the rest of my life, unless i buy something.

With his irreverent and sometimes politically incorrect humor, Jackie Mason attracts just as many people who adore him as hate him. Although born in Wisconsin, he grew up as Yacov Moshe Maza in New York City. Descended from a long line of rabbis, he was ordained in 1958 but realized that his place was not on the bimah of a synagogue but on the stage of a theater. He began work as a teenage busboy at Borscht Belt resorts rising to social director while perfecting his brand of comedy. His big break came when he was older and began appearing on television variety shows. He was a frequent guest on the popular *Ed Sullivan Show* until one specific appearance in 1964. During the performance, Mason received a signal to cut his act short. Sullivan thought Mason responded with an obscene gesture on the air. Whether he did or not, Mason's career came to a sudden halt. He still made appearances in clubs, in films, and onstage. But it was only when he introduced a one-man Broadway show in 1986, *The World According to Me!* that his career took off again. Never one to stay away from controversy, he continued to inflame racial, political, and social tensions with succeeding shows that he performed all over the country.

Don Rickles

Born: May 8, 1926, New York, New York

It's not really stand-up comedy. I don't tell jokes. It's a lot of emotion and attitude.

Don Rickles has made a career out of insulting people. No one was immune from his sharp-tongued but good-natured barbs. While he often targeted audience members, he reserved his best insults for his show business friends. He once said, "If I were to insult people and mean it, that wouldn't be funny." His original goal was to become a serious actor, and indeed, over his long career, he appeared in a number of films including *Run Silent, Run Deep* (1958), *Enter Laughing* (1967), and as the voice of Mr. Potato Head in *Toy Story* (1995) and *Toy Story 2* (1999). He was a friend of Frank Sinatra, who became one of his greatest supporters in spite of being the frequent target of Rickles's humor. "Make yourself at home, Frank. Hit somebody." Beginning in 1959, Rickles became a popular performer in Las Vegas, Nevada, nightclubs. He also made many appearances on television shows. He is well known for his charitable work including the raising of funds for the Barbara and Don Rickles Gymnasium at Sinai Temple in Los Angeles.

Allan Sherman

Born: November 30, 1924, Chicago, Illinois
Died: November 20, 1973, Los Angeles, California
Real name: Allan Copelon

Allan Sherman won great acclaim for his hilarious parodies, with Jewish overtones, of hit songs. His best known and most often performed is "Hello, Muddah, Hello, Fadduh!" a song about experiences at summer camp. He was born Allan Copelon and, in spite of a difficult childhood, found his niche as a musician and composer. He entered show business as a television show producer but began experimenting with parody songs. Friends recommended him to a recording company, and *My Son, the Folksinger* became a hit in 1962. In that album, he put humorous lyrics to popular folk songs. With the success of his first album, a new career was launched as he wrote humorous lyrics for existing tunes. For the famous "With a Little Bit of Luck" from *My Fair Lady*, he substituted, "With a Little Bit of Lox;" for "Seventy-Six Trombones" from *The Music Man*, he wrote, "Seventy-Six Sol Cohens"—"Seventy-Six Sol Cohens in the country club/And a hundred and ten nice men named Levine." His parodies became increasingly popular, and he served as an inspiration to other comics including Bill Cosby and Weird Al Yankovic. He made frequent television guest appearances and wrote several successful books. His comedy was often dependant on current events, and as those events disappeared from public interest, so did interest in his parodies. As his popularity faded, Sherman, always a heavyset man, developed diabetes and emphysema. He died at the age of forty-eight.

Phil Silvers

Born: May 11, 1911, Brooklyn, New York
Died: November 1, 1985, Century City, California
Real name: Fischl Silver

Phil Silvers began his theatrical career at the age of eleven, singing in theaters to fill in time when film projectors broke down. Two years later, he left school and embarked on a professional vaudeville career. He developed a stage personality as a loud wise guy while performing in burlesque houses and in early talking movies. He won the Tony Award for his acting in a popular 1952 Broadway play, *Top Banana*. During his career, he was featured in dozens of popular films including *A Funny Thing Happened on the Way to the Forum* (1966) and *It's a Mad, Mad, Mad, Mad World* (1963). Silvers is best known for his portrayal of a fast-talking gambler and swindler, U.S. Army sergeant Ernest G. Bilko, on the long running 1950s television sitcom, *The Phil Silvers Show*.

The Three Stooges

Moe Howard

Born: June 19, 1897, Brooklyn, New York
Died: May 4, 1975, Los Angeles, California
Real name: Moses Horwitz

Larry Fine

Born: October 5, 1902, Philadelphia, Pennsylvania
Died: January 24, 1975, Woodland Hills, California
Real name: Louis Feinberg

Shemp Howard

Born: March 17, 1895, Brooklyn, New York
Died: November 23, 1955, Hollywood, California
Real name: Samuel Horwitz

Curly Howard

Born: October 22, 1903, Brooklyn, New York
Died: January 18, 1952, San Gabriel, California
Real name: Jerome Horwitz

Joe Besser

Born: August 12, 1907, Saint Louis, Missouri
Died: March 1, 1988, Hollywood, California

Curly-Joe DeRita

Born: July 12, 1909, Philadelphia, Pennsylvania
Died: July 3, 1993, Woodland Hills, California
Real name: Joe Wardell

Over time, there were actually six men who portrayed the Three Stooges. Beginning in 1934, they were featured in more than two hundred short films, which were shown as fillers in movie theaters between featured films. Their popularity grew when the films were released to television in 1958. The Stooges became the number one children's entertainers on the air. Although the film plots changed, the contents remained constant. Slapstick, violent humor, poking, and hitting were the Stooges's trademarks. Each stooge had his own personality. The original Stooges were Larry, Moe, and Shemp. When Shemp left the act, his place was taken by his brother, Curly. When Curly left the act because of illness in 1946, Shemp returned and remained until his death in 1955. Shemp was replaced by Joe Besser who, in turn, was replaced by the final stooge, Curly-Joe DeRita.

From left: **Larry Fine, Curly Howard, and Moe Howard**

Of all the Stooges, Larry, Moe, and Curly were the most popular. Moe, with his bowl haircut, was the "boss stooge," who gave the orders and was usually the first to inflict pain on the others. Curly, whose head was actually shaved, was a rotund wise guy. His famous high-pitched phrases, "N'yuk! N'yuk!" and "Woo-woo-woo!" were mimicked for years by children. Larry, identified by his frizzy hair, appeared as the only sane member of the group and the butt of physical and verbal attacks. They really didn't hurt one another, but the use of visual tricks and well-timed sound effects made viewers (especially parents) cringe.

Ed Wynn

Born: November 9, 1886, Philadelphia, Pennsylvania
Died: June 19, 1966, Beverly Hills, California
Real name: Isaiah Edwin Leopold

Ed Wynn was a classic vaudeville comic. He created a number of onstage characters that became the focus of his act. Perhaps the most lasting was the Perfect Fool, in which he told jokes in a giggly, high-pitched voice. He became a star of the Ziegfeld Follies in 1914 wearing his silly hat—a size too

small. He used a variety of visual props, many of which he invented, including a windshield wiper to be served with juicy grapefruit. In the 1930s, he starred in a popular radio show wearing a fireman's helmet to reflect his role as the Texaco fire chief. He believed in authenticity and always appeared before radio studio audiences in costume and used his old vaudeville props while telling jokes on the air. In the late 1940s and early 1950s, he hosted his own television show, but his reluctance to hire writers led to his running out of jokes. He left the program but continued to make guest appearances on other network shows and began a new career as a serious actor in plays and films. He best described his own career when he said that a comedian is not a man who says funny things but rather someone who says things funny.

ACT III:
On Fire

Times change and with it the styles of comedy. What tickled the funny bones of early twentieth-century immigrants had little comic effect on their descendants decades later. The corny slapstick of the vaudeville era gave way to the puns and jokes of radio comedians, which in turn gave way to television comedy sitcoms. While there always were—and will continue to be—funny carryovers from one generation to another, something unique began happening in the 1960s. Comedians began looking at political and cultural events of the times and replacing old-fashioned humor with biting and sarcastic material.

The mood of the United States was changing. The McCarthy era of the 1950s still cast a shadow over the country a decade later. Wisconsin senator Joseph McCarthy had embarked on an uncontrolled public attack on people and institutions he accused of promoting Communism in the United States. An unwritten state of self-censorship enveloped the nation. Entertainers and comics were careful about what they said lest they too be accused of being pro-Communist. In the 1960s, with the United States involved in the unpopular Vietnam War (1957–1975), thousands of people, including university students, began to publicly protest on campuses and in the streets. It was the era of hippies—mainly young people who were developing their own liberal counterculture in response to the conservative larger culture. They were reacting to the "squeaky clean" image of the United States portrayed in television programs such as *Leave It to Beaver* and *Father Knows Best*. Those programs featured all-white, happy, middle-class families leading "perfect" lives in suburbia clueless about the racial and social upheaval that was taking place around them. For young comedians of that era, those events provided the fuel to fire up their careers. But before they would become household favorites on television, they earned their reputations in front of smaller audiences.

Stand-up comedy was nothing new. That's what Jewish comedians had been doing on vaudeville stages and in the Borscht Belt for decades. What was new in the 1960s were their topics. Moving away from traditional one-liners and slapstick, the young comics began poking fun at the world around them with humor, sometimes offensive or provocative, on a higher intellectual level. They began performing in specialty nightclubs that welcomed newcomers and provided them with a training ground. Clubs such as the hungry i and the Purple Onion in San Francisco and Catch a Rising Star in New York became the models for others in cities as wide spread as Chicago and Los Angeles. Audiences in those clubs did not find the same humor they were used to seeing in movie theaters or on television. The leader of this new wave of comedians was Mort Sahl. He was the first to make "nightclubs safe for political satire, rabid social commentary, and bleak and black humor." Sahl was soon imitated by others. A new form of comedy developed that replaced the mainstream acts of the past. Within a decade, comedy clubs sprang up in cities around the country and became popular gathering spots for up-and-coming comedians. The clubs gave rise to famous names in comedy including Lenny Bruce, Gilda Radner, Jerry Seinfeld, Lewis Black, and Sarah Silverman. Their comedy styles were markedly different

In 1978 comedy stars *(from left)* Steve Martin, David Brenner, and Gilda Radner show their support for upcoming comics at New York City's Catch a Rising Star.

from that of Jack Benny or Groucho Marx. Profanity often punctuated their commentary, and they freely talked about controversial issues including religion and sex. But the audience for these new humorists was limited to the seating capacities of the individual clubs. In 1975 that changed when *Saturday Night Live* went on the air with a style that was based on the new forms of comedy, yet acceptable to a large television audience. It featured a number of Jewish comedians including Jon Lovitz, Gilda Radner, and Adam Sandler. They were not afraid to satirize Jewish themes. By the 1990s, another iconic television show with Jewish themes captivated Americans. Jerry

Seinfeld had been a successful stand-up comedian who took his irreverent "show about nothing" into comedy stardom. As in Jack Benny's radio and television shows decades earlier, *Seinfeld* was a show about the "real" life of a comedian. Where it differed was in the constant use of Jewish subthemes even by cast members who portrayed non-Jewish characters. In an interview in *New York Magazine*, Seinfeld said, "Superman is my role model. I have this very romantic image of the stand-up comic, the solitary challenge of being out there on your own, using whatever you have on you. Every man thinks of himself as a low-level superhero. And it came true for me. I got to do what I wanted to do in life. To me, that's being Superman."

From left: **George (Jason Alexander), Elaine (Julia Louis-Dreyfus), Kramer (Michael Richards), and Jerry (played by Seinfeld himself), hang out at their local diner in a 1992 episode of *Seinfeld*.**

Jewish comedians also made their mark in films during this period. They brought the flavor of stand up comedy to wildly successful movies. Woody Allen and Mel Brooks drew upon their long experiences as comedy writers to create films with biting humor based on Jewish themes. In *Blazing Saddles*, Mel Brooks has a Native American chief speaking Yiddish, and in *Annie Hall*, Allen imagines himself as a stereotyped Hasidic Jew, sitting at the Easter dinner table of his girlfriend's family. Jewish comedy was fully Americanized and accepted.

The twenty-first century brought the rise of the viral video, an often humorous short film available on the Internet and

Mel Brooks plays the part of a Yiddish speaking Indian chief in his 1974 movie *Blazing Saddles*.

popularized through links. On sites such as Facebook, Funny or Die, and YouTube, users can easily share links with their friends, creating a whole new kind of buzz for comedians. Videos like Sarah Silverman's "The Great Schlep" urged young voters to visit their bubbies and zadies in Florida and encouraged them to vote for Barack Obama. Fans of *Saturday Night Live* and *The Daily Show* can view sketches on the shows' websites when they miss an episode. Thanks to the Internet, comedians can quickly and easily reach fans by posting videos on the Internet, rather than waiting for their next film to be released or TV show to air.

Biographies

Testing the Limits

Roseanne Barr

Born: November 3, 1952, Salt Lake City, Utah

Coming from a traumatic childhood, Roseanne Barr became a popular comedian in comedy clubs and on television. She was hurt in an automobile accident at the age of sixteen and spent a year in a hospital recovering. She never returned to high school. Instead, she moved away and worked as a waitress, tossing wisecracks and funny comments at customers. She enjoyed going to comedy clubs and decided to shake up the all-male world she saw in front of the microphone. Her style of comedy was confrontational and brassy, and she developed a reputation as a tough but funny performer. Her big break occurred with an appearance on

Experts say you should never hit your children in anger. When is a good time? When you're feeling festive?

The Tonight Show in 1985, which led to engagements in clubs around the country. Her most popular routines centered on making fun of family life and chores. Using those routines as a model, she starred on the ABC television network in her own situation comedy show, *Roseanne*, about a working-class family. She told a reviewer, "I want to do real revolutionary TV...a show that reflects how people really live." The show remained popular for eight years despite the fact that her rough edges and unrestrained behavior caused her problems professionally and personally.

Lenny Bruce

Born: October 13, 1925, Mineola, New York
Death: August 3, 1966, Hollywood, California
Real name: Leonard Alfred Schneider

There are no dirty words, only dirty minds.

In the 1950s and 1960s, Lenny Bruce shocked audiences with his freewheeling and sometimes obscene club acts. No subject was off-limits to him. Whether speaking about religion or politics, his style of humor attracted attention, not always positive. Following his idol, Mort Sahl, he became known as a founder of the "sick" comedy style. His parents divorced when he was a small boy, and he was raised by relatives. He served in the U.S. Navy during World War II and upon his release headed to California to study acting. He moved back to New York to work in nightclubs as a stand-up comic. With the passage of time, his act evolved from impressions and parodies to outspoken and controversial rantings. He was arrested several times for drug possession and obscenity. In 1964, after a performance in which he used more than one hundred obscene words, the courts found his performances "patently offensive to the average person" and sentenced him to jail. His career went into a decline from that point.

Andrew Dice Clay

Born: September 29, 1957, Brooklyn, New York
Real name: Andrew Clay Silverstein

I'm so terrific I even have my own toll-free number: 1-800-PERFECT.

Andrew Dice Clay followed in the footsteps of Lenny Bruce to become the most daring comic of the 1990s. His obscenity-laced acts were provocative. No group was spared from his biting humor. At a time when the United States was becoming more sensitive to its treatment of minorities and the disabled, Clay targeted them for parody and ridicule. His audiences loved him. He began his career as an impressionist, and his humor was clean. Gradually, he transformed his standard vcharacterization into the rough and crude "Diceman"—his trademark. Even as he gained professional exposure in film and in comedy clubs, his profanity earned him the distinction in 1989 of being banned for life from the MTV cable channel. He always insisted that "it's not me up there—it's an act."

Billy Crystal

Born: Long Beach, New York, March 14, 1947

Billy Crystal is a comedic actor whose films and television and stage appearances have made him one of America's favorite entertainers. His father owned a well-known music store in New York and was a promoter and friend of jazz musicians, many of whom befriended young Billy. After college he gave up on his original hope of becoming a professional baseball player and began to work in television and in comedy clubs.

In high school, I was the class comedian as opposed to the class clown. The difference is, the class clown is the guy who drops his pants at the football game; the class comedian is the one who talked him into it.

His big break into show business occurred when he starred in *Soap*, a TV parody of soap operas that aired from 1977 to 1981. Later, he joined *Saturday Night Live* in 1984, bringing with him his talent for impersonations honed in earlier stage acts and television shows. "You look maaahvelous!"—an exaggerated phrase associated with Crystal's act— became widely popular throughout the country. He went on to star in a number of comedies, including *When Harry Met Sally* (1989), *City Slickers* (1991), and as the voice of one-eyed monster Mike Wazowski in *Monsters, Inc* (2001). Crystal's ease with working in front of live audiences led to his semiautobiographical, Tony Award-winning one-man show, *700 Sundays*, which he took to Broadway in 2004 and then to theaters around the country. His book, based on his performance with the same title, became a best seller.

Andy Kaufman

Born: January 17, 1949, New York, New York
Died: May 16, 1984, Los Angeles, California

Unlike other comedians, Andy Kaufman never told a joke. His style of comedy seemed weird to many who watched his performances, first in improvisational comedy clubs and later on television. He grew up in Great Neck, New York, and began entertaining other kids at birthday parties when he was nine years old. The word *eccentric* comes to mind when describing his brand of comedy. He would stand in front of an audience and just read out loud on and on from a novel or hire buses to take an entire Carnegie Hall audience for milk and cookies after a performance. He developed a character he called

Foreign Man, who spoke poor English with a European accent and seemed naive and clueless. That character was transformed into his popular portrayal of Latka Gravas on the hit television show *Taxi* from 1978 to 1983. That role furthered his comedy career and led to film roles and guest appearances on other television shows. During those years he astounded his fans by touring around the country as a professional wrestler who only fought women and never lost. In his only match with a man before a television audience, Andy ended up in the hospital. He appeared more than fifteen times on *Saturday Night Live*. *Andy's Funhouse*, a 1979 television special, featured some of his best-known sketches. He died in 1984 at the age of thirty-five of lung cancer. He best summed up his career by saying, "There's no way to describe what I do. It's just me."

Jon Lovitz

Born: July 21, 1957, Tarzana, California

I heard you call me immature earlier. Well, you're just a big poop head.

Jon's start in show business began in college, where he studied acting and appeared in a number of plays. After graduation, he went to New York but had no success in finding a job, so he returned to Los Angeles, where he began appearing in comedy clubs. It was only in 1985, when he was hired for *Saturday Night Live*, that his career took off. As a cast member and writer for five years, he developed memorable characters including Master Thespian and Hanukkah Harry. After leaving the show, he used his unique vocal style in a number of animated films and advertisements. He was promoted as "the man who invented the Yellow Pages" and, for Subway, he was the voice (and face) that told viewers to "eat fresh!" Lovitz was a popular guest on numerous television sitcoms including *Seinfeld* and *Friends* and appeared in films such as *¡Three Amigos!*, *Big*, and *City Slickers II*. In 2007 he opened his own comedy club in San Diego, which continues to feature many of his comedian friends.

Gilda Radner

Born: June 28, 1946, Detroit, Michigan
Died: May 20, 1989, Los Angeles, California

Best known for her roles on *Saturday Night Live* between 1975 and 1980, Gilda Radner honed her comedy skills as a member of a Canadian improvisational comedy group. She worked with other young soon-to-be popular comics like John Belushi and Bill Murray. During her five years on *Saturday Night Live,* she portrayed a number of memorable characters such as Roseanne Roseannadanna and Baba Wawa, patterned after well-know television news reporter Barbara Walters. After leaving *Saturday Night Live*, Gilda appeared in several films and television programs. She married fellow Jewish comedian Gene Wilder in 1984. Sadly, in 1986, she was diagnosed with ovarian cancer and passed away three years later.

Just goes to show ya—it's always somethin'!
— Roseanne Roseannadanna

That was so funny, I forgot to LAFFF!
— Gilda Radner as Lisa Lupnor

Joan Rivers

Born: June 8, 1933, Brooklyn, New York
Real name: Joan Molinsky

I'm Jewish. I don't work out. If God wanted us to bend over he'd have put diamonds on the floor.

Joan Rivers's father was a physician, and she grew up in a well-to-do family. Even as a child, she knew that she wanted a career in show business but "convincing others was a hard part." After graduating from Barnard College, she began working for the Lord & Taylor department store. After a failed first marriage, she decided to launch her career as a stand-up comedian. Traveling around the country, she performed in improvisational comedy clubs, including Chicago's Second City. Rivers featured anecdotes about her Jewish upbringing, her love of shopping, and her reluctance to do housework. She often jokes about her numerous plastic surgeries to improve her looks over the years. When she married again, her husband, Edgar, became the butt of many jokes in her act. Since the late 1960s, she has hosted several television talk shows of her own and appeared as a frequent replacement host on *The Tonight Show*. Her trademark line is "Can we talk?" Her love of fashion led her to create her own very successful line of women's jewelry. In the past few years, drawing on her knowledge of fashion, she became a witty and often sarcastic commentator on fashion for the major awards shows such as the Academy Awards and the Emmys.

They usually have two tellers in my local bank, except when it's very busy, when they have one.

Rita Rudner

Born: September 17, 1953, Miami, Florida

At a time when many comedians rely on edgy and X-rated humor, Rita Rudner reflects the low-key comedy of her idols, Jack Benny and Woody Allen. She entered show business not as a comedian but as a dancer in leading Broadway musicals such as *Follies* and *Annie*. In her mid-twenties, she realized that the number of female dancers greatly outnumbered female comics and decided on a career change. She began with appearances in comedy clubs and worked her way up to appearances on *The Tonight Show* with Johnny Carson. "I like to take people away from the real world," she once said, "because the real world is a very complicated, upsetting place. I don't want to make anyone upset. I'll just make you laugh." Today, Rita performs almost exclusively before live audiences in Las Vegas. Since 2001 more than one million people have seen her perform there.

Mort Sahl

Born: May 11, 1927, Montreal, Canada

Mort Sahl became an inspiration to an entire generation of American comedians. He was a great improviser who could engage audiences with his comments on contemporary social problems and news events. He did not hold back with comments about elected leaders in Washington. His biting sarcasm and wit was appreciated by the audiences at the comedy clubs, and Sahl soon became famous. In 1960 his picture appeared on the front cover of *Time* magazine, which wrote a feature story about him. With the assassination of President John F. Kennedy in 1963, Sahl's irreverent political humor fell out of favor. His career took another direction as he appeared in plays; wrote a book on his life, *Heartland*; and released recordings of his humor.

Gene Wilder

Born: June 11, 1933, Milwaukee, Wisconsin
Real name: Jerome Silberman

A lot of comic actors derive their main force from childish behavior. Most great comics are doing such silly things; you'd say, "That's what a child would do."

Born Jerome Silberman, Wilder's show business career began on the stage when he was still in college. He trained at a number of acting schools and received several early important roles on Broadway and in film. His 1971 portrayal of Willy Wonka in *Willy Wonka and the Chocolate Factory* earned him positive notice. His performance in Mel Brooks's film *The Producers*, resulted in an Academy Award nomination. He starred in several other Mel Brooks comedies, including portraying a young rabbi in *Blazing Saddles* (1974), and the title character in *Young Frankenstein* (1974). He married comedian Gilda Radner in 1984, and after her sudden death in 1989, he helped found Gilda's Club to combat ovarian cancer. In the past few years, he turned his talents to writing romantic novels. His second book, *The Woman Who Wouldn't*, was published in 2008.

Biographies

Comedy 2.0

Lewis Black

Born: August 30, 1948, Washington, D.C.

> Religion is like stand-up comedy because they both draw their biggest audiences on the weekends and they both provide a sense of comfort.

"America's foremost commentator on everything," is the way Lewis Black refers to himself. Known for his angry rantings on politics and modern society, he became a favorite on Jon Stewart's *The Daily Show*, the Comedy Central channel, and HBO. He began his career as a playwright and has since published books on politics and humor and recorded several comedy albums. His association with Comedy Central led to a number of programs on cable and parts in several films, including *Accepted* (2006) and *Unaccompanied Minors* (2006). He is an active touring stand-up comedian, particularly popular on college campuses, in clubs and indie venues, and theaters that spotlight edgy acts.

Sacha Baron Cohen

Born: October 13, 1971, London, England

Is Disneyland a part of the UN?
—Sacha Baron Cohen as Ali G

His early background gives no indication that Sacha Baron Cohen would become a premier comedian. He was a serious student whose Jewish roots took him to Israel for a year of work on a kibbutz. He returned to London where he studied history at Cambridge University. After graduation he began experimenting with comic characters, and when he discovered that his talent for mimicry actually drew laughs, he began a career in comedy. His characterizations assumed their own identities into which he totally immersed himself. For all intents, he literally became the character. His first character, developed in London, was flashy gangster Ali G, who interviewed unsuspecting people in a manner that made them appear silly or unknowing. This character made its way across the Atlantic where he interviewed American personalities who had no idea they were talking to someone whose sole intent was to make them look foolish. His most shocking character was Borat Sagdiyev, a fictional reporter for Kazakhstan television. Borat was sexist, anti-Semitic, and clueless about American life. Baron Cohen, Jewish himself, said that his intent was to ridicule anti-Semitism and hatred of all kinds. In 2006 his film *Borat: Cultural Learnings of*

America for Make Benefit Glorious Nation of Kazakhstan became an instant comic hit. Not everyone got the joke, however. In 2008 he announced that he was retiring the character of Borat. Raised in an observant Orthodox family, Baron Cohen still keeps kosher and observes Shabbat. He recently had a daughter with Australian actress Isla Fisher, who converted to Judaism.

Larry David

Born: July 2, 1947, Brooklyn, New York

Anyone can be confident with a full head of hair. But a confident bald man—there's your diamond in the rough.

Starting as a stand-up comedian, Larry David quickly discovered that his real talent was behind the scenes, as a writer. Claiming that he used his own life experiences for the sketches he wrote, much of his comedy centered on awkward social situations. He was the cocreator and writer of the successful *Seinfeld* television show. Some say that he was the model for the whiny, insecure character of George Constanza on the show. After *Seinfeld* ended, David returned to center stage in his own show, *Curb Your Enthusiasm*, playing himself. The show was unique in that it was only loosely scripted, drawing upon ad-lib conversations and actions to create humor.

Al Franken

Born: May 21, 1951, New York, New York

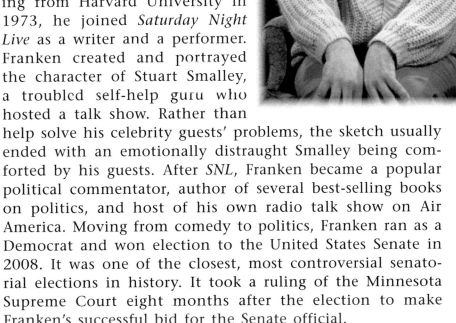

> I'm good enough, I'm smart enough, and doggone it, people like me.
> —Al Franken as Stuart Smalley

Much of Franken's humor focuses on political subjects and politicians, and his liberal views often infuriate conservatives. His career began as a stand-up comedian in Minneapolis, Minnesota, where he grew up. After graduating from Harvard University in 1973, he joined *Saturday Night Live* as a writer and a performer. Franken created and portrayed the character of Stuart Smalley, a troubled self-help guru who hosted a talk show. Rather than help solve his celebrity guests' problems, the sketch usually ended with an emotionally distraught Smalley being comforted by his guests. After *SNL*, Franken became a popular political commentator, author of several best-selling books on politics, and host of his own radio talk show on Air America. Moving from comedy to politics, Franken ran as a Democrat and won election to the United States Senate in 2008. It was one of the closest, most controversial senatorial elections in history. It took a ruling of the Minnesota Supreme Court eight months after the election to make Franken's successful bid for the Senate official.

Judy Gold

Born: November 15, 1962, Newark, New Jersey

Judy Gold graduated from Rutgers University in 1984 with the intent of embarking on a career as a music teacher. On a fluke, she began doing stand-up comedy and began a successful show business career. She has been a writer, producer, and performer. She was the producer of *The Rosie O'Donnell Show* for a number of years. Her one-woman shows performed on Broadway and around the country have been particularly popular. A common theme revolves around being Jewish. Her book, *25 Questions for a Jewish Mother*, depicts her warm but funny relationship with her own mother.

We never talked, my family. We communicated by putting Ann Landers newspaper advice articles on the refrigerator.

Adam Sandler

Born: September 9, 1966, Brooklyn, New York

> I sing seriously to my mom on the phone, to put her to sleep. I have to sing "Maria" from West Side Story. When I hear her snoring, I hang up.

Sandler developed a cast of lovable fictional characters on *Saturday Night Live,* which were perfect vehicles for his offbeat, often childish style of humor. He also wrote for the show and contributed several songs about uncommon topics such as the school lunch lady. Although born in New York, he grew up in Manchester, New Hampshire. Sandler began his show business career while still a student at New York University. He worked at comedy clubs before being "discovered" by *Saturday Night Live,* which gave his career a jump start. His classic "Hanukkah Song" provided Americans with a comic look at who was Jewish in popular culture. "Some people think Ebenezer Scrooge is/ Well, he's not, but guess who is?/ All Three Stooges." In the 1990s, he began a successful film career by portraying lovable but goofy characters in films such as *Billy Madison* (1995), *Happy Gilmore* (1996), and *Big Daddy* (1999). He founded Happy Madison Productions, which produces comedies in the vein of Sandler's childish humor, including *Bedtime Stories* (2008) and *Paul Blart: Mall Cop* (2009).

In 2008 Sandler cowrote and starred in *You Don't Mess with the Zohan*, a comedy about a former Israeli intelligence agent pursuing his dream of becoming a hairstylist in New York City. Though the film received mixed reviews, it solidified Sandler's status as a high-grossing movie star and showed Hollywood a comical side of Israel.

Jerry Seinfeld

Born: April 29, 1954, Brooklyn, New York

Seinfeld, the television show, was a phenomenal success, still enjoyed in reruns. Many consider it one of the best comedy shows ever. It revolved around fictional escapades of the real Jerry Seinfeld and his group of loyal and quirky friends. The "show about nothing" took simple everyday experiences and turned them into humorous half-hour stories. Many of the incidents were based on actual happenings in the lives of Seinfeld and the program's cocreator, comedian Larry David. One episode deals with purchasing rye bread. Another focuses on a long wait to be seated at a Chinese restaurant, while another devotes the half hour to an incident with a dry cleaner. Jerry Seinfeld grew up on Long Island, outside of New York City, enjoying the work of television comedians. After graduating from Queens College, he sought a career as a stand-up comedian. He developed a low-key form of humor that dealt with everyday life. He practiced his craft in front of audiences at comedy clubs, and his storytelling style became popular. As he perfected his act, he continually learned from other comics while supporting himself with a series of menial jobs. To further his career, he moved to Los Angeles and gradually earned an appearance

It's amazing that the amount of news that happens in the world everyday always just exactly fits the newspaper.

on *The Tonight Show* in 1981, which launched his career. He began traveling around the country performing his popular stand-up comedy at clubs and universities. In 1989 he sat down with Larry David in a New York diner. What emerged from their conversation was the idea for a television show. *Seinfeld* was born. While Jerry would play himself, Jason Alexander took the role of his friend George, modeled after the real-life Larry David. Michael Richards played the role of Kramer, based on the life of a real Kramer who was once Larry David's neighbor. Julia Louis-Dreyfus was the fourth member of the close-knit group of fictional friends. The show was a spectacular hit from 1990 to 1998. At the height of its continued popularity, Seinfeld decided to go out on a high and end the show. It has been in syndication since, and viewers around the world can still enjoy the humor. Since the program ended, Jerry has been busy writing books and renewing his stand-up work.

Sarah Silverman

Born: December 1, 1970, Bedford, New Hampshire

Sarah Silverman's words often take on the appearance of being bigoted and insensitive. That's precisely what she intends. Following in the tradition of Mort Sahl and Lenny Bruce, her sharp-tongued stand-up comedy targets ethnic and minority groups with particular emphasis on Jews. She grew up in a proud Jewish family (one of her sisters is a rabbi) and has no hesitation of lampooning the Holocaust. Silverman began her career as a writer and performer for one year on *Saturday Night Live* and quickly moved on to appear in several films and on television comedy programs. Controversy has always followed her career. In 2001 she created a furor with an appearance on *Late Night with Conan O'Brien* when she used a derogatory word for Asians on the air. She created and performed in a one-woman show called *Jesus Is Magic*, which was also made into a movie. She got her own series on Comedy Central, *The Sarah Silverman Program*, playing herself in a situation comedy. The popular show featured her typical offensive remarks. She remains a popular comedian who frequently appears on talk shows and in concert. During the 2008 presidential election, she created a video, "The Great Schlep," encouraging Jewish young people to influence their aged grandparents in Florida to vote for Barack Obama.

Jon Stewart

Born: November 28, 1962, Trenton, New Jersey
Real name: Jonathan Stuart Leibowitz

If you watch the news and don't like it, then [The Daily Show] is your counter program to the news.

Jon Stewart's *The Daily Show* is broadcast every evening on Comedy Central at the same time that local television stations air their nightly news reports. Unlike those programs, Stewart's show has a comic twist. Many viewers tune in his show believing that Stewart's clever blending of real news with his own wry humor actually provides a deeper insight into the day's happenings. He was born Jonathan Stuart Leibowitz but changed his name when he found that people had difficulty pronouncing it. Growing up, he amused his family with his humor and graduated from high school as the student with the best sense of humor. His reputation followed him to the College of William and Mary, where the soccer team established the Leibo Award in his honor, presented annually to the team's funniest member. After college he worked at a number of odd jobs until his first stand-up appearance at a New York comedy club. In the 1990s, he began working in television as a program host and writer. By 1993 he was hosting *The Jon Stewart Show* on MTV, which was distinguished by its inclusion of offbeat guests and discussions. He was a guest host on *The Late Late Show* and the *The Larry Sanders Show* and became a sought-after presenter at awards shows. He was the host of several Academy Awards shows. Comedy Central's *The Daily Show* was already on the air for two years when Stewart began hosting it in 1999. Since then the "fake news" show has gone on to win several journalism awards and ten Emmys for Stewart as a writer and producer.

Ben Stiller

Born: November 30, 1965, New York City

Even as a child, Ben Stiller knew he was bound for a career in show business. His parents, Jerry Stiller and Anne Meara, were well-known comedians and actors who often included their son in public appearances. At the age of eight, he and his sister played violin on a popular television talk show. When he was ten years old, he used a Super 8 camera to begin making films. This interest in behind-the-camera work

If my parents were, like, plumbers, who knows what I would be doing?

eventually resulted in his successful career as a film director, writer, and producer. His show business career actually began on the Broadway stage as a performer in the Tony Award–winning show, *The House of Blue Leaves*. He spent his spare time working on short film spoofs of popular films. These films caught the eye of writers at *Saturday Night Live* and MTV, earning Stiller national attention at both venues. His first major film role was in *Empire of the Sun* (1987) directed by Steven Spielberg. Ben's early television shows focused on parody. They were popular with young indie audiences, but not with critics. He became a full-fledged film star with his appearances in *Meet the Parents* (2000), *Zoolander* (2001), *Dodgeball: A True Underdog Story* (2004), and *Tropic Thunder* (2008). In 2000 he married actress Christine Taylor, who appeared with him in several films. The couple has two children.

SOURCE NOTES

Numbers refer to page numbers where quotations appear

4 Jewish Publication Society of America, *Tanakh: The Holy Scriptures* (Philadelphia: Jewish Publication Society, 1985), 29.

4 Irv Saposnik, "These Serious Jests: American Jews and American Comedy," *Judaism*, Summer 1998, 320.

4 Lawrence J. Epstein, *The Haunted Smile* (New York: Public Affairs, 2001), x.

4 Jeff Berkowits, "What's with Jewish Comedy," *San Diego Jewish Journal*, August 2004, 15.

8 Irving Howe, *World of Our Fathers* (New York: Schocken, 1989), 402.

11 Stefan Kanfer, "The Buckle on the Borscht Belt," *Gentleman's Quarterly*, August 1985, 147.

12 Morey Amsterdam, quoted in David Stout, "Morey Amsterdam, Comedian and Joke Encyclopedia, Dies," *New York Times*, October 30, 1996, D22.

13 Fanny Brice, quoted in Haythum R. Khalid, "Famous Quotes about Audiences," *Book of Famous Quotes*, 2009, http://www.famous-quotes.com/topic.php?tid=88 (January 19, 2009).

14 Fanny Brice, quoted in Jim Cox, *The Great Radio Sitcoms* (Jefferson, NC: McFarland, 2007), 65.

14 Geoffrey Petty, *Teaching Today: A Practical Guide* (Cheltenham, UK: Nelson Thornes, 2004), 427.

15 Molly Picon, *Molly: An Autobiography* (New York: Simon and Schuster, 1980), 301.

16 Molly Picon, quoted in Willian Schack, "Article," *New York Times*, November 4, 1931.

18 Joseph Weber and Lew Fields, quoted in Esther Romeyn and Jack Kugelmass, *Let There Be Laughter: Jewish Humor in America* (Chicago: Spertus Press, 1997), 30.

20 Henny Youngman, *Take My Wife, Please!* (New York: Morrow, 1991), 11.

22 Norman H. Finkelstein, *Sounds in the Air: The Golden Age of Radio* (New York: Scribners, 1993), 13.

26 Ibid., 44.

26 Ibid.

28 Mel Tolkin, quoted in Margalit Fox, "Mel Tolkin, Lead Writer for 'Show of Shows,' Dies at 94," *New York Times*, November 27, 2007.

29 Epstein, 138.

30 Woody Allen, quoted in Michael Moncur, "Quotations Details," *QuotationsPage.com*, 2007, http://www.quotationspage.com/quote/41.html (January 19, 2009).

31 Jack Benny, quoted in Michael Moncur, "The Quotations Page," *QuotationsPage.com*, 2007, http://www.quotationspage.com/quote/311.html (January 19, 2009).

32 Jack Benny, quoted in Richard F. Shepard, "Jack Benny, 80, Dies of Cancer in Beverly Hills," *New York Times*, December 26, 1974, 9.

33 Milton Berle, quoted in BrainyMedia.com, "Candlelight Quotations," *BrainyQuote*, 2009, http://www.brainyquote.com/words/ca/candlelight140831.html (January 20, 2009).

37 Mel Brooks, quoted in Michael Moncur, "Quotation Details," *QuotationsPage.com*, 2007, http://www.quotationspage.com/quote/26750.html (January 20, 2009).

42 Eddie Cantor, quoted in Michael Moncur, "Quotation Details," *QuotationsPage.com*, 2007, http://www.quotationspage.com/quote/1355.html (January 20, 2009).

45 Danny Kaye, quoted in BrainyMedia.com, "Candlelight Quotations," *BrainyQuote*, 2009, http://www.brainyquote.com/quotes/quotes/d/dannykaye314792.html (January 20, 2009).

47 Jerry Lewis, quoted in Amy Wallace, "Jerry Lewis (Comedian 79, Las Vegas). What I've Learned (Interview)," *Esquire*, January 2006, 82.

49–50 Time, "Horse Feathers," *Time Partners with CNN*, 2009, http://www.time.com/time/magazine/article/0,9171,744191,00.html (January 21, 2009).

52 Don Rickles, quoted in Gary Strauss, "Insult Master Rickles Isn't Warm, but He's Hot," *USA Today*, November 30, 2007, 8E.

58 Ed Wynn, quoted in Charles N. Pollak II, "Ed Wynn Advocates Clean Humor and 'Philosophy of a Fool' . . . Giggles Way to Peace in 'Hooray for What?'" *Harvard Crimson*, November 8, 1937, 1.

61 Gerald Nachman, *Seriously Funny: The Rebel Comedians of the 1950s and 1960s.* (New York: Knopf, 2003), 10.

63 Jerry Seinfeld, quoted in Chris Smith, "City Slicker: Jerry Seinfeld Spins a New York State of Mind into TV's Funniest, Smartest Sitcom, *New York Magazine*, February 3, 1992, 33.

66 Rosanne, quoted in Andy Barker, "Heard the One About . . . ?" *Guardian* (London), March 12, 2006, 21.

35 Lenny Bruce, quoted in Michael Moncur, "Quotation Details," *QuotationsPage.com*, 67, http://www.quotationspage.com/quote/33842.html (January 20, 2009).

68 Andrew Dice Clay, as Ford Fairlane, in *The Adventures of Ford Fairlane,* quoted in *Jim Silverstein, Movie Quotes to Get You Through Life* (Morrisville, NC: lulu.com, 2007), 20.

69 Billy Crystal, quoted in TV.com, "Billy Crystal Blurbs," *TV.Com*, n.d., http://www.tv.com/billy-crystal/person/1041/trivia.html (January 20, 2009).

71 Andy Kaufman, quoted in JVLNet Internet Services, "A Brief History of Significant Events in the Public Life of Andy Kaufman," *JVLNet*, October 3, 1995, http://andykaufman.jvlnet.com/aktime.htm (January 21, 2009).

72 Jon Lovitz, quoted in IMDB, "Biography for John Lovitz," *IMDB: The Internet Movie Database*, n.d., http://www.imdb.com/name/nm0001484/bio (January 21, 2009).

74 Joan Rivers, quoted in Irv T. Saposnik, "These Serious Jests: American Jews and Jewish Comedy," *Judaism*, Summer 1998, 317.

75 Rita Rudner, quoted inBrainyMedia.com, "Rita Rudner Quotes," *BrainyQuote*, 2009, http://www.brainyquote.com/quotes/authors/r/rita_rudner.html (January 20, 2009).

75 Rita Rudner, interview by John Blackstone, CBS News, May 4, 2008.

76 IMDb.com, "Mort Sahl," *IMDb: The Internet Movie Database*, n.d., http://www.imdb.com/name/nm0756340/ (January 21, 2009).

77 Gene Wilder, quoted in Brian Baiker, "Young Frankenstein's Memoir," *Newsweek*, May 18, 2005, http://www.newsweek.com/id/48951 (January 20, 2009).

78 Lewis Black, quoted in Kelli Skye Fadroski, "Lewis Black Gets Religion in His New Book," *Orange County Register*, June 26, 2008, 16.

79 Sacha Baron Cohen, as Ali G, quoted in AllGreatQuotes.com, "Ali G Quotes," *All Great Quotes*, 2008, http://www.allgreatquotes.com/ali_g_quotes.shtml (January 20,2009).

80 Larry David, quoted in BrainyMedia.com, "Larry David Quotes," *BrainyQuote*, 2009, http://www.brainyquote.com/quotes/authors/l/larry_david.html (January 20, 2009).

81 Al Franken as Stuart Smalley, quoted in Michael Moncur, "Quotation Details," *QuotationsPage.com*, 2007, http://www.quotationspage.com/quote/31725.html (January 20, 2009).

82 Judy Gold, quoted in Ann Wanderman, "2000 Quotations by Women," *LDResources*, February 14, 2000, http://www.ldresources.org/etext/quotations_women.doc (January 20, 2009).

83 Adam Sandler, quoted in Think Exist.com Quotations, "Adam Sandler Quotes," *Think Exist.com*, n.d., http://en.thinkexist.com/quotes/adam_sandler/ (January 21, 2009).

85 Jerry Seinfeld, quoted in Think Exist.com Quotations, "Jerry Seinfeld Quotes," *Think Exist.com*, n.d., http://thinkexist.com/quotation/it-s_amazing_that_the_amount_of_news_that_happens/209752.html (January 21, 2009).

86 Sarah Silverman, quoted by Dave Itzkoff, "Sarah Silverman's Message to Your Grandma—Vote Obama," *New York Times*, October 7, 2008, C1.

87 Jon Stewart, quoted in TV Guide Online, "Daily Show with Jon Stewart," *TV Guide.com*, January 20, 2009, http://www.tvguide.com/tvshows/daily-jon-stewart/191468 (January 20, 2009).

88 IMDb.com, "Awards for Jon Stewart." *IMDb: the Internet Movie Database*, 2009, http://www.imdb.com/name/nm0829537/awards (January 31, 2009).

89 Ben Stiller, quoted in American-Israeli Cooperative Enterprise, "Ben Stiller, 1965–," *Jewish Virtual Library*, 2009, http://www.jewishvirtuallibrary.org/jsource/biography/Stiller.html (January 20, 2009).

SELECTED BIBLIOGRAPHY

Ausubel, Nathan. *A Treasury of Jewish Folklore.* New York: Crown, 1963.

Epstein, Lawrence J. *The Haunted Smile.* New York: Public Affairs, 2001.

Finkelstein, Norman H. *Sounds in the Air: The Golden Age of Radio.* New York: Scribners, 1993.

Howe, Irving. *World of Our Fathers.* New York: Schocken, 1989.

Jewish Publication Society of America. *Tanakh: The Holy Scriptures.* Philadelphia: Jewish Publication Society, 1985.

Katkov, Norman. *The Fabulous Fanny: The Story of Fanny Brice.* New York: Knopf, 1953.

Nachman, Gerald. *Seriously Funny: The Rebel Comedians of the 1950s and 1960s.* New York: Knopf, 2003.

Petty, Geoffrey. *Teaching Today: A Practical Guide.* Cheltenham, UK: Nelson Thornes, 2004.

Picon, Molly. *Molly: An Autobiography.* New York: Simon and Schuster, 1980.

Romeyn, Esther, and Jack Kugelmass. *Let There Be Laughter: Jewish Humor in America.* Chicago: Spertus Press, 1997.

Youngman, Henny. *Take My Wife, Please!* New York: Morrow, 1991.

INDEX

Norman H. Finkelstein is the author of seventeen nonfiction books for young readers. Two of them, *Heeding the Call: Jewish Voices in America's Civil Rights Struggle* and *Forged in Freedom: Shaping the Jewish-American Experience* won National Jewish Book Awards. His biography of Edward R. Murrow, *With Heroic Truth*, received the Golden Kite Honor Award for Nonfiction. His earlier Kar-Ben titles are *Ariel Sharon, Friends Indeed* and *Theodor Herzl: Architect of a Nation*. A resident of Framingham, Massachusetts, Finkelstein is a retired public school librarian and a longtime faculty member in the Prozdor High School of Hebrew College.

PHOTO ACKNOWLEDGMENTS

The images in this book are used with the permission of: © Elizabeth Simpson/Taxi/Getty Images, backgrounds on pp. 1, 5, 12, 22, 30, 60, 66, 78; © Photofest, p. 6; Billy Rose Theatre Division, The New York Public Library, Astor, Lenox and Tilden Foundations, p. 9; AP Photo/Irving Desfor, p. 10; Everett Collection, pp. 12, 13, 18, 25, 31, 37, 39, 47, 49, 52, 53, 57, 64; Library of Congress, pp. 14 (LC-DIG-ggbain-38802), 17 (LC-USZ62-126199); © General Photographic Agency/Hulton Archive/ Getty Images, p. 15; CSU Archives/Courtesy Everett Collection, p. 19; © Harold M. Lambert/Hulton Archive/Getty Images, p. 23; © Camerique/ClassicStock/The Image Works, p. 28; AP Photo, pp. 30, 40; © NBC Television/Hulton Archive/Getty Images, p. 33; NBCU Photo Bank via AP Images, pp. 35, 51, 73; Goldwyn/United Artists/The Kobal Collection, p. 42; © Michael Ochs Archives/Getty Images, p. 44; Mirrorpix/Courtesy Everett Collection, p. 45; © Ralph Morse/Time & Life Pictures/ Getty Images, p. 55; © Hulton Archive/Getty Images, p. 58; © Tim Boxer/Hulton Archive/Getty Images, p. 62; © Columbia TriStar Television/Courtesy Everett Collection, p. 63; © HBO/Courtesy Everett Collection, p. 66; George Konig/Rex Features USA, p. 67; © Steve Snowden/Getty Images, p. 68; AP Photo/Wally Fong, p. 69; © PBS/Courtesy Everett Collection, p. 71; © Giulio Marcocchi/ Getty Images, p. 72; © DMI/Time & Life Pictures/Getty Images, p. 74; © Ethan Miller/Getty Images, p. 75; © Robert W. Kelley/Time & Life Pictures/Getty Images, p. 76; © Silver Screen Collection/ Hulton Archive/Getty Images, p. 77; © Paul Hawthorne/Getty Images, p. 78; © Jeffrey Mayer/ WireImage/Getty Images, p. 79; © Amy Sussman/Getty Images, p. 80; © NBC/Courtesy Everett Collection, p. 81; © Jemal Countess/WireImage/Getty Images, p. 82; Alan Singer/NBCU Photo Bank via AP Images, p. 83; © Michael Grecco/Getty Images, p. 85; © Michael Bezjian/WireImage/Getty Images, p. 86; © Brad Barket/Getty Images, p. 87; © Vince Bucci/Getty Images, p. 89.

Front Cover: AP Photo/Matt Sayles. Back Cover: © Elizabeth Simpson/Taxi/Getty Images.